GALATIANS

REFORMED EXPOSITORY BIBLE STUDIES

A Companion Series to the Reformed Expository Commentaries

Series Editors

Daniel M. Doriani
Iain M. Duguid
Richard D. Phillips
Philip Graham Ryken

Daniel: Faith Enduring through Adversity
Galatians: The Gospel of Free Grace
James: Portrait of a Living Faith

GALATIANS

THE GOSPEL OF FREE GRACE

A 13-LESSON STUDY

REFORMED EXPOSITORY
BIBLE STUDY

JON NIELSON

P.O. BOX 817 • PHILLIPSBURG • NEW JERSEY 08865-0817

CONTENTS

SERIES INTRODUCTION

Studying the Bible will change your life. This is the consistent witness of Scripture and the experience of people all over the world, in every period of church history.

King David said, "The law of the LORD is perfect, reviving the soul; the testimony of the LORD is sure, making wise the simple; the precepts of the LORD are right, rejoicing the heart; the commandment of the LORD is pure, enlightening the eyes" (Ps. 19:7–8). So anyone who wants to be wiser and happier, and who wants to feel more alive, with a clearer perception of spiritual reality, should study the Scriptures.

Whether we study the Bible alone or with other Christians, it will change us from the inside out. The Reformed Expository Bible Studies provide tools for biblical transformation. Written as a companion to the Reformed Expository Commentary, this series of short books for personal or group study is designed to help people study the Bible for themselves, understand its message, and then apply its truths to daily life.

Each Bible study is introduced by a pastor-scholar who has written a full-length expository commentary on the same book of the Bible. The individual chapters start with the summary of a Bible passage, explaining **The Big Picture** of this portion of God's Word. Then the questions in **Getting Started** introduce one or two of the passage's main themes in ways that connect to life experience. These questions may be especially helpful for group leaders in generating lively conversation.

Understanding the Bible's message starts with seeing what is actually there, which is where **Observing the Text** comes in. Then the Bible study provides a longer and more in-depth set of questions entitled **Understanding the Text**. These questions carefully guide students through the entire passage, verse by verse or section by section.

It is important not to read a Bible passage in isolation, but to see it in the wider context of Scripture. So each Bible study includes two **Bible Connections** questions that invite readers to investigate passages from other places in Scripture—passages that add important background, offer valuable contrasts or comparisons, and especially connect the main passage to the person and work of Jesus Christ.

The next section is one of the most distinctive features of the Reformed Expository Bible Studies. The authors believe that the Bible teaches important doctrines of the Christian faith, and that reading biblical literature is enhanced when we know something about its underlying theology. The questions in **Theology Connections** identify some of these doctrines by bringing the Bible passage into conversation with creeds and confessions from the Reformed tradition, as well as with learned theologians of the church.

Our aim in all of this is to help ordinary Christians apply biblical truth to daily life. **Applying the Text** uses open-ended questions to get people thinking about sins that need to be confessed, attitudes that need to change, and areas of new obedience that need to come alive by the power and influence of the Holy Spirit. Finally, each study ends with a **Prayer Prompt** that invites Bible students to respond to what they are learning with petitions for God's help and words of praise and gratitude.

You will notice boxed quotations throughout the Bible study. These quotations come from one of the volumes in the Reformed Expository Commentary. Although the Bible study can stand alone and includes everything you need for a life-changing encounter with a book of the Bible, it is also intended to serve as a companion to a full commentary on the same biblical book. Reading the full commentary is especially useful for teachers who want to help their students answer the questions in the Bible study at a deeper level, as well as for students who wish to further enrich their own biblical understanding.

The people who worked together to produce this series of Bible studies have prayed that they will engage you more intimately with Scripture, producing the kind of spiritual transformation that only the Bible can bring.

Philip Graham Ryken
Coeditor of the Reformed Expository Commentary
Author of *Galatians* (REC)

INTRODUCING GALATIANS

Galatians is the epistle of free grace. Its **main purpose** is to bring freedom from bondage to any works of the law—freedom that can only come through faith in Jesus Christ. This liberating purpose was well summarized by the fourth-century Roman scholar Gaius Marius Victorinus, writing in his later years, after he had finally put his personal trust in Christ: "The Galatians are going astray because they are adding Judaism to the gospel of faith in Christ. Disturbed by these tendencies, Paul writes this letter in order that they may preserve faith in Christ alone."[1]

The **author** of Galatians introduces himself in the very first verse. It is Paul, the famous evangelist, missionary, and church planter, who wrote the majority of the letters that we read in the New Testament. In fact, this may have been the first biblical epistle that the apostle wrote. From the outset, he is agitated and alarmed—much more so than in any of his other epistles. This is because, to his amazement and astonishment, some of the churches that he had helped to start were under serious theological attack and thus in danger of abandoning a biblical understanding of their salvation. To address this error, Paul impatiently and somewhat angrily mounts a vigorous defense of his authority as an apostle and of the accuracy of the gospel that he preached in Galatia. He was not some second-rate apostle with a secondhand gospel, as some of his critics were saying. On the contrary, the good news he preached came straight from God.

The precise **audience** for Paul's epistle is somewhat difficult to determine. At first glance, it is easy enough to see that Paul wrote his letter to "the churches of Galatia" (1:2). The trouble is that in Roman times "Galatia"

---

1. Gaius Marius Victorinus, quoted in Leland Ryken, Philip Ryken, and James Wilhoit, *Ryken's Bible Handbook* (Wheaton, IL: Tyndale, 2005), 524.

referred to several different and sometimes overlapping regions in Asia Minor, and it is not entirely certain how Paul was using the term. To give a contemporary analogy, it would be like someone writing a letter to "the churches in Carolina," without specifying North or South Carolina. Possibly Paul was writing to churches in the Roman province of Galatia—churches in cities such as Iconium, Lystra, and Derbe, which Paul had visited on his first missionary journey (Acts 14). Other scholars suggest that the apostle wrote Galatians after his second missionary journey, to churches in north-central Galatia.

In any case, the **context** for Paul's letter is clear enough. At first, the Galatian Christians had eagerly embraced the good news about Jesus Christ (see Acts 13–14). But apparently a group of Jewish-Christian missionaries had come along later to tell Gentiles in Galatia that in order fully to belong to Christ, they had to receive the Old Testament sign of circumcision (the removal of the male foreskin; see the covenant that God made with Abraham in Genesis 17:9–14). The doctrinal position of these "Judaizers," as they are sometimes called, is conveniently summarized in Acts 15:1: "Unless you are circumcised according to the custom of Moses, you cannot be saved." As far as Paul was concerned, this teaching was causing a theological crisis. He rightly saw that making circumcision mandatory was a form of legalism that would undermine the freedom of the gospel.

It is important to understand that the Judaizers did not deny that justification came by faith. However, by adding works to faith—instead of trusting only in Christ—they did deny the vital biblical doctrine of justification by faith *alone*. As a result, they were guilty of preaching another gospel, when in fact there is no other gospel. Here is how John Stott describes the situation: the Judaizers "did not deny that you must believe in Jesus for salvation, but they stressed that you must be circumcised and keep the law as well. In other words, you must let Moses finish what Christ has begun. Or rather, you yourself must finish, by your obedience to the law, what Christ has begun."[2]

There are several well-known passages in the book of Galatians, but perhaps the **key verse** is chapter 2, verse 16: "We know that a person is not

---

2. John R. W. Stott, *The Message of Galatians*, The Bible Speaks Today (Downers Grove, IL: InterVarsity, 1968), 22.

justified by works of the law but through faith in Jesus Christ, so we also have believed in Christ Jesus, in order to be justified by faith in Christ and not by works of the law, because by works of the law no one will be justified." Paul could hardly be more emphatic. Not once, not twice, but *three times* in one verse he declares that we are justified by faith (or trust) in Christ. And not once, not twice, but *three times* he insists that we cannot be justified (that is, declared righteous) before the bar of God's justice by doing works of the law. Such repetition is the Bible's way of adding exclamation points. Paul doesn't want the Galatians or anyone else to miss his point: the way to get right with God is not by doing good works, but by trusting completely in what Jesus has done—specifically, what Jesus has done by living a righteous life, dying an atoning death, and rising from the grave with the power of eternal life.

Justification by grace alone, through faith alone, in Christ alone, is the central doctrine of Galatians, but the book contains other vital **theological themes** as well. Galatians has as much to say about the Holy Spirit as it does about Jesus Christ—specifically, the work of the Holy Spirit in sanctifying believers who are justified by faith. Nor is justification the only important aspect of salvation that is discussed in Galatians. Paul's letter also teaches basic truths about adoption (by the gift of the Holy Spirit, every child of God is able to call God "Father" and will receive an eternal inheritance; see 4:6–7), redemption (we have been rescued from slavery through the payment of a price; see 3:13), and union with Christ (through baptism, every believer is joined to Jesus and becomes one with his body, the church; see 3:28). Once we understand salvation properly, we can also come to a better understanding of the law, which is a curse to sinners who cannot keep it, but becomes a blessing to believers by showing us our need for Christ. The law exposes our guilt, so that we can see our need for a Savior.

Like everything else in Scripture, Galatians was written for our spiritual benefit. In considering the book's **practical application**, a good place to start is by admitting that we are all legalists at heart. Even if the sign of circumcision is no longer a live issue for most of us, it is still tempting to think that there is something we can do to make ourselves good enough for God—or at least to put ourselves more in his favor.

Galatians was written to liberate us from any form of performance-based religion. Whenever we try to improve our standing with God by observing religious rituals, doing charitable deeds, or performing pious acts of devotion, we are placing a surcharge on God's free grace. The good news is that God accepts us simply on the merits of Jesus Christ. We do not receive this gift of grace by doing anything for ourselves, but simply by trusting in what Jesus has done. We cannot earn God's favor; it only comes free. Rather than needing to justify ourselves, therefore, we are justified by Jesus.

Once we put our trust in Christ—specifically, in his death and resurrection—we are free to live a life that is more pleasing to God. First, we must be crucified with Christ (2:20); then we must put to death our old sinful nature, with its unholy passions and ungodly desires (5:24). The goal is "faith working through love" (5:6)—a life that is free from sins of the flesh (5:16–21) and full of the fruit of the Spirit instead (5:22–23). In other words, liberty should never become an excuse for license; it should always lead us into a life of loving service to others instead.

The letter to the Galatians has had a life-changing impact for many people who lived in spiritual bondage and wanted to be set free. Alongside Romans, Galatians is the biblical book that launched the Protestant Reformation by liberating a monk named Martin Luther from works righteousness and helping him rediscover the doctrine of justification by faith alone. Thankfully, Luther was not the last person to be set free by Paul's most passionate epistle. "With its trumpet-call to Christian freedom," Galatians "has time and again released the true gospel from the bonds in which well-meaning but misguided people have confined it so that it can once more exert its emancipating power in the life of mankind, empowering those who receive it to stand fast in the freedom with which Christ has set them free."[3]

To understand the flow of Galatians, it may be helpful to keep a **simple outline** in mind. In the first two chapters (1:1–2:21), Paul shares his *spiritual autobiography* and defends his gospel of free grace by asserting his independent authority as an apostle. In the next two chapters (3:1–4:31), he makes his *theological argument* and explains his gospel of free grace with a series of biblical and theological examples. Finally, in the last two chapters (5:1–6:18), Paul gives an *ethical exhortation* to live a free and holy life by keeping in step with the Holy Spirit. To provide a little more detail:

---

3. F. F. Bruce, *The Epistle to the Galatians*, New International Greek Testament Commentary (Grand Rapids, MI: Eerdmans, 1982), 278.

Introduction
  Salutation (1:1–5)
  Denunciation (1:6–10)

Personal: The Autobiography of an Authentic Apostle
  Paul's Conversion (1:11–17)
  Paul's First Visit to Jerusalem (1:18–24)
  Paul's Second Visit to Jerusalem (2:1–10)
  Paul's Rebuke of Peter (2:11–14)
  Paul's Life as a Justified Sinner (2:15–21)

Doctrinal: The Gospel of Free Grace
  The Experience of the Galatians (3:1–5)
  The Example of Abraham (3:6–9)
  Justification by Faith, not Works (3:10–14)
  The Difference between Law and Promise (3:15–25)
  From Slavery to Sonship (3:26–4:11)
  An Appeal to Trust Paul's Message (4:12–20)
  The Allegory of Hagar and Sarah (4:21–31)

Practical: Living Free in Christ
  Exhortation to Freedom from Circumcision (5:1–12)
  Living by the Spirit, Not Giving In to License (5:13–26)
  Bearing People's Burdens and Other Good Works (6:1–10)

Conclusion and Benediction (6:11–18)

Philip Graham Ryken

LESSON 1

NO OTHER GOSPEL

Galatians 1:1–10

THE BIG PICTURE

In some ways, Paul's opening remarks to the Galatian believers are typical of all his epistles sent to churches. He identifies himself as an apostle; he speaks words of "grace and peace" to them; he affirms a common faith in Jesus Christ, to the glory of God. But the letter does not proceed with any specific commendation (as there is in the opening verses of Philippians, for example), and the pleasantries end abruptly! Paul launches into a stinging rebuke with intense and emotional language: "I am *astonished . . .*" (Gal. 1:6). He goes on to use some of the strongest language of any of his epistles to cast judgment on those who would preach "a different gospel" (v. 6), calling for such opponents of Christ to be "accursed" (v. 8). The apostle is identifying a major problem—a radically dangerous affront to the faith of the believers to whom he writes. Any gospel that is contrary to the one preached by the apostles is a road away from Jesus Christ himself. Particularly pernicious are the distortions of the gospel that take away from the sufficiency of the finished work of Jesus Christ on the cross, the benefits of which are received by faith alone.

Read Galatians 1:1–10.

GETTING STARTED

1. Have you ever received a stern rebuke from someone you love and trust? How did it feel? How was the rebuke ultimately helpful?

2. Consider any experience in which you have distinguished something that is fake, or counterfeit, from something real. What are some of the best ways to identify a counterfeit?

OBSERVING THE TEXT

3. Compare and contrast the first few verses of Philippians and Ephesians with the first few verses of Galatians. What do you notice that is unique or noteworthy about Paul's greeting in Galatians? What about the opening section (beginning with verse 6), after the greeting?

The Importance of Galatians, pg. 4

Paul's epistle to the Galatians has been called the Magna Carta of Christian liberty. Its theme verse is a declaration of independence: "We know that a person is not justified by works of the law but through faith in Jesus Christ" (Gal. 2:16). Whenever the church has understood this gospel message, Galatians has brought life and freedom to recovering Pharisees.

4. How would you describe Paul's general tone in these opening verses of the letter? If you had to ascribe an emotion to this section, what would it be? What specific words or phrases from the text lead you to answer that way?

5. What hints do you get about the Galatian churches' context, just from these opening verses? What influences, people, and/or teachings seem to be present in their community?

UNDERSTANDING THE TEXT

6. What does Paul say about himself? To whom is the letter addressed? Why might it be significant that Paul is writing to "churches" (plural) in Galatia? See 1:1–2.

7. Look at verse 1 and then at verse 10 (the first and last verses of this opening section). What common phrases or ideas are present? Why do you think Paul is so intent—right at the beginning of this letter—to contrast a gospel ministry that is from man with one that is from Christ?

8. What problem is Paul addressing in verses 6–9? What does he say about the true gospel? Why does he think that the Galatians are moving in a direction that is so terribly dangerous?

9. How can Paul be so confident that the gospel he preached to the Galatians was true? How does verse 10 help to answer that question?

10. Paul does not specifically define or explain the gospel in this passage, although he will do so later in the letter. Take a moment and read Galatians 2:15–21. What are the key elements of the gospel of Christ, preached by Paul, that he emphasizes in those verses? What seem to be the elements, or core teachings, of the "different gospel" that Paul opposes, according to that passage?

Dangerous Judaizers, pg. 9

Religious traditionalists, probably from Jerusalem, were trying to teach the Galatians a new gospel. These men dogged Paul's footsteps all over Asia Minor. Often they are called the "Judaizers" because they wanted to require Gentiles to follow Jewish customs. . . . In short, their gospel was Jesus Christ plus the law of Moses.

BIBLE CONNECTIONS

11. Paul is, from the opening verses of this epistle, pushing back on the influence of false teachers who are sometimes called "Judaizers." These men sought to bring Christians under the rule of the Jewish law. Read 1 Samuel 15:22–23 and Psalm 40:6–8. What clues do these Old Testament passages give us about the insufficiency of merely keeping the law?

12. Read Hebrews 7:23–28. According to this passage, what is the perfect and final salvation that is offered through the gospel of Jesus Christ? Why, given what is described in Hebrews 7, would it be so foolish to go back to being under the law?

THEOLOGY CONNECTIONS

13. As you may know, one of the rallying cries of Martin Luther and the other Reformers of the sixteenth century was *sola fide* ("by faith alone"). How might Galatians have been a key letter for shaping the convictions of the Reformers? How might their passion and zeal have been similar to Paul's? How might they have seen the gospel of Jesus Christ being distorted in their day?

14. In the Westminster Confession of Faith, we find this statement about justification by faith: "Those whom God effectually calleth, He also freely justifieth: not by infusing righteousness into them, but by pardoning their sins, and by accounting and accepting their persons as righteous; not for any thing wrought in them, or done by them, but for Christ's sake alone" (11.1). Discuss the importance of this teaching. How does this teaching connect to the central concern Paul has about the false gospel being promoted to the Galatian believers?

APPLYING THE TEXT

15. In what ways might some people (even well-meaning people) "distort the gospel" of Jesus Christ, or even preach/teach a "different" gospel? What motivations tend to drive such teachers? What appeals to their followers? What examples of this might we see in the church today?

16. What can we learn from Paul's intense and angry reaction to the Galatians' desertion of the gospel of Jesus Christ? How can his passion guide and shape our convictions about guarding the pure gospel of Jesus Christ?

17. In what ways are you personally tempted to drift from the gospel of
     Jesus Christ? How are you prone to legalism, or the impulse to try
     to earn favor with God through what you do? How are you prone to
     embrace "cheap grace," relying on God's forgiveness without pursuing
     obedience and godliness?

PRAYER PROMPT

Consider ways that you are tempted to forget the gospel of Jesus Christ
and salvation through faith in him alone. Pray that this study in Galatians
would lead you to a stronger embrace of the true gospel. Pray for wisdom
and clarity to recognize other gospels or distortions of the true gospel.

A Counterfeit Gospel, pg. 21

The church's greatest danger is not the anti-gospel outside the church;
it is the counterfeit gospel inside the church. The Judaizers did not walk
around Pisidian Antioch wearing T-shirts that said, "Hug me, I'm a false
apostle." What made them so dangerous was that they knew how to talk
the way Christians talk . . . [but] they did not have the gospel after all.

LESSON 2

AUTOBIOGRAPHY OF A GOSPEL FREEDOM FIGHTER

Galatians 1:11–2:10

THE BIG PICTURE

One way to think about the structure of Galatians is to divide it into three main parts: *autobiography* (chapters 1–2), *theology* (chapters 3–4), and *ethics* (chapters 5–6). As you read and study this passage, then, you are right in the midst of the autobiographical section. The Judaizers who had been ravaging the Galatian churches with the false gospel of justification by works had to dismiss Paul's *apostleship*, as well as his *apostolic message*. Once they could undermine his authority, they could cast doubt on his gospel. This is precisely why Paul begins, in this section, by recounting his personal testimony. He goes back to his conversation, and then describes the growth of his gospel ministry during the early years of his Christian preaching. Paul is fiercely defending his apostleship, even as he will soon go on to defend his apostolic gospel message. In this passage, we hear the great apostle describe and defend his own spiritual autobiography. Paul's point is clear: I was saved by God in Christ, set apart as an apostle by God in Christ, and the gospel I preach comes directly from God in Christ!

Read Galatians 1:11–2:10.

GETTING STARTED

1. Why is it so important to know people before you entrust yourself to them—or even believe what they say? What experiences have you had with trusting someone's *words*, only after you have come to know him or her as a *person*?

2. An *ad hominem* argument (Latin for "to the man") is an argument in which the main topic of discussion is avoided, as one party seeks to attack the character or integrity of the other party making an argument. How have you seen *ad hominem* arguments used? Why can they sometimes be effective, even if they are not logically valid?

OBSERVING THE TEXT

3. Notice the dominance of first person pronouns in this part of Paul's letter. What does this tell you about Paul's focus in this passage? Why might this focus on himself be so important as he begins this letter to the Galatians?

Paul's Apostleship, pg. 26
Paul understood that people had to accept his apostleship before they would accept his gospel.

4. Who are some of the specific people that Paul mentions in this passage? What are some of the specific places that he mentions? Why might both of these (people and places) be important to the argument he is making?

5. As you initially read through the passage, what hints do you get about the strategies of Paul's opponents? To what kinds of attacks does he allude and seek to respond?

UNDERSTANDING THE TEXT

6. Why is it so important for Paul to insist that he did not receive the gospel "from any man" (1:12)? What does this affirmation have to do with his role as an apostle?

7. What argument is Paul making, as he describes his journeys after his conversion (1:17–18), as well as his meetings with Peter (Cephas) and James (1:18–20)? What accusation from his opponents does he seem to be answering?

8. What seems to have motivated Paul to visit Jerusalem (2:1–2)? Why was Titus an important test case for the interactions and confrontations he had there (2:3)?

9. As Paul goes on to describe his visit to Jerusalem, how does he describe the influence of the Judaizers that he confronted there (2:4–5)? How does Paul describe his ultimate victory in the midst of the Jewish believers in Jerusalem (2:7–10)?

10. How was this entire episode in Jerusalem a key affirmation of Paul's gospel ministry to the Gentiles? How does his recounting of this incident further establish the credibility and legitimacy of his role as an apostle?

Freedom Fighter, pg. 40

Whatever we call these men, they were enemies of freedom, which is why Paul took such a strong stand against them: "to them we did not yield in submission even for a moment, so that the truth of the gospel might be preserved for you" (Gal. 2:5). Paul was a freedom fighter. He knew that people who want to keep their freedom in Christ have to fight for it.

BIBLE CONNECTIONS

11. Take a moment and read Jeremiah 1:4–5. How do Paul's words in Galatians 1:15–16 echo the words in Jeremiah? Why might this be significant? What might Paul be signaling about the significance and legitimacy of his gospel ministry and preaching?

12. Now read Mark 6:1–3. On what basis do the people from Jesus' hometown reject his teaching and preaching? How might Paul be sharing in the sufferings of Jesus, even as he defends himself against the Judaizers?

THEOLOGY CONNECTIONS

13. Read Galatians 1:13–16 one more time. Why was Paul's conversion and apostolic call so utterly astounding and unexpected? What can we infer about God, as we consider Paul's conversion? What are the implications for our own relationships with God?

14. The Westminster Confession of Faith says this about "effectual calling": "All those whom God hath predestinated unto life, and those only, He is pleased, in His appointed and accepted time, effectually to call, by

His Word and Spirit, out of that state of sin and death, in which they are by nature to grace and salvation, by Jesus Christ; enlightening their minds spiritually and savingly to understand the things of God, taking away their heart of stone, and giving unto them an heart of flesh; renewing their wills, and, by His almighty power, determining them to that which is good, and effectually drawing them to Jesus Christ: yet so, as they come most freely, being made willing by His grace" (10.1). How is this doctrinal statement illustrated by the experience of the apostle Paul?

APPLYING THE TEXT

15. In what ways do you struggle with confidence in the reliability of Scripture and/or the message of the gospel of Jesus Christ? How can this passage strengthen your faith in God and the reliability of the apostolic gospel?

16. How is freedom in the gospel of Jesus Christ most likely to be challenged in our context today? What might the influence of the "Judaizers" look like in the twenty-first-century church, as extra requirements are added to the free gospel of grace through Jesus Christ?

17. What can we learn from the apostles' meetings and conversations with Paul (described in 2:1–10) that could guide our conversations with fellow believers today? How might this guide us in the midst of questions, or even disagreements?

PRAYER PROMPT

As you conclude your study of this passage, take some time to consider the wonder of Paul's conversion and call—as well as the miracle of your own! Thank God for his effectual call—for the way he made your dead heart come alive to repentance and faith in his Son. After all, if you are in Christ, then you are holding onto the very same gospel that was so fiercely defended by Paul as coming directly from the God of grace! Finally, spend some time asking God to strengthen you to stand courageously against teachings, influences, and impulses within your own heart that would do damage to the free gospel of grace.

Paul's Endorsement, pg. 46
The apostles . . . acknowledged Paul's commission to preach the gospel. . . . The right hand of fellowship was more than a handshake. It was a symbolic gesture of partnership in the gospel. It showed that in the division of their labor, the other apostles endorsed Paul's mission to the Gentiles.

LESSON 3

PAUL, PETER, AND THE
FIGHT FOR THE GOSPEL

Galatians 2:11–21

THE BIG PICTURE

As Paul continues the autobiographical section of his letter, which proves and establishes his apostleship, he looks back on a time when he actually had to confront another apostle: Peter. Recounting this interaction for his audience is part of his argument; for Paul to have the authority to rebuke Peter certainly establishes his legitimacy and authority! But this recollection quickly leads Paul into a beautiful summary of the gospel of grace, as he goes on to explain precisely why it was so important for him to confront Peter's behavior. Peter's drawing back from eating with the Gentile believers at Antioch was about more than just ethnic tensions and differences: Paul saw it as a failure to grasp all of the implications of the gospel of grace. For Paul, Peter's actions demonstrated that the doctrine of *justification by faith, and not by works,* needed to be courageously defended in public. Hence Paul's well-known words: "We know that a person is not justified by works of the law but through faith in Jesus Christ" (Gal. 2:16). The Christian who is saved by faith has died to the law—and to self—and now lives completely by faith for Jesus Christ the Lord.

Read Galatians 2:11–21.

31

GETTING STARTED

1. We hear a lot about peer pressure, especially in the context of the teenage years. Why is peer pressure so powerful? What can it look like for adults—in a variety of contexts?

2. In what areas of life are we sometimes asked to justify ourselves to others? Why is the impulse to earn favor, or prove ourselves to others (and to God), so deeply ingrained in our hearts?

OBSERVING THE TEXT

3. What do you notice about Paul's recollection of his confrontation with Peter (2:11–15)? Is this conflict between two apostles surprising to you? Why or why not?

Courage and Cowardice, pg. 56

What Peter did was not a matter of principle; it was a case of cowardice. . . . From this we learn that even great Christians can fall into sin, sometimes more than once. We also learn how necessary it is for Christian ministers to have the courage to defend the gospel against all opposition, including opposition that comes from within the church.

4. If you could pick one theme verse for this passage after your initial reading, what would it be? Why?

5. List and explain some of the arguments and/or accusations that Paul seems to be responding to in this passage. Try to identify some of the opposing voices that Paul and his readers are hearing.

UNDERSTANDING THE TEXT

6. Why would Paul speak about his confrontation with Peter at this point of the letter (2:11)? How does his recollection of this event explain his commitment to the gospel of grace, but also further establish his credibility as an apostle of God?

7. What seems to have motivated Peter to draw back from eating with the Gentiles (2:12)? What was the negative effect that Peter's actions had on those around him (v. 13)? On what basis did Paul rebuke Peter (v. 14), and why is this so important for the continued advance of the gospel to all peoples?

8. Read Galatians 2:16 again. Why is this such a foundational statement for understanding the essence of the gospel of grace that Paul preached? How does this statement radically contradict the teaching of the Judaizers? How is it connected to Paul's confrontation of Peter, recounted in the preceding verses?

9. What kind of accusations or attacks from the Judaizers might Paul be responding to in 2:17? Read Romans 6:1–4. How is Paul responding to a similar attack in that passage?

10. In what sense were the Judaizers (and Peter, temporarily) attempting to "rebuild" the law (2:18)? Why does Paul see this as so dangerous? In what sense have we "died" to the law as Christians (v. 19) and been "crucified with Christ" (v. 20)? How does life "by faith" in Jesus motivate us toward an even more complete righteousness than the law (vv. 20–21)?

The Cross and the Christian Life, pg. 73
But here is the surprise: if you are a follower of Christ, then *you* were nailed to the cross too! The crucifixion is not just a fact about the life of Christ and a momentous event in human history, but is also part of every Christian's personal life story.

BIBLE CONNECTIONS

11. Paul's account of his confrontation with Peter is not the only record in Scripture of Peter being rebuked. The gospel writers show us Peter's early refusal to accept the suffering and death of Jesus as a crucial part of his mission (see Mark 9:31–33) and the stern rebuke that he received from Jesus. How can Peter's own weaknesses, failures, and growth encourage us as we grow in our understanding and application of the gospel?

12. Paul's teaching on justification by faith, apart from works, actually should not have struck the Jewish believers as new. As Paul shows in Romans 4, Genesis demonstrates that the father of the Jewish faith, Abraham, was himself justified by faith—before the law had even been given to God's people. Read Genesis 15:1–6; how does Abraham demonstrate faith in God?

THEOLOGY CONNECTIONS

13. The Westminster Shorter Catechism defines God's act of justification in this way: "Justification is an act of God's free grace, wherein he pardoneth all our sins, and accepteth us as righteous in his sight, only for the righteousness of Christ imputed to us, and received by faith alone" (Q&A 33). How is that doctrine clearly taught by Paul in this passage

from Galatians? Why is this doctrine tremendously life-giving and freeing for us as redeemed sinners?

14. Many in the Reformed tradition have pointed out one powerful use of the Old Testament law (among others): it clearly demonstrates our sinfulness and our need for God's grace. The Heidelberg Catechism tells us that the law is preached "so that throughout our life we may more and more become aware of our sinful nature, and therefore seek more eagerly the forgiveness of sins and righteousness in Christ" (Q&A 115). How is this declaration helpful to you in expanding your understanding of the law of God?

APPLYING THE TEXT

15. In what ways are you currently tempted by those around you (as Peter was) to abandon the radical demands of the gospel? How can you be more diligent to fight these temptations? Do any of these temptations spring from your ethnic or religious community or context?

16. How are you, even right now, tending toward self-justification, or trying to earn God's favor, in your relationship with him?

17. What can you do to avoid the common tendency toward treating God's grace as "cheap grace" (a pardon for sin that does not demand obedience and devotion)? How can Paul's teaching about being dead to the law, but alive to Christ, help to motivate you toward obedience and godliness in the days ahead?

PRAYER PROMPT

As you move toward a time of prayer after your study of this passage, consider a few potential topics. First, ask God to reveal tendencies in your life and heart to respond to peer pressure, which would lead you to compromise your commitment to Jesus Christ and his gospel. Second, pray that God would protect you from attempts at self-justification, on the one hand, but also from cheap grace, on the other. Ask him to give you strength, by his Spirit, to enable you to live more and more in righteous obedience to the crucified and risen Savior.

Crucified with Christ, pg. 76
The Christian life is like life after death. We were crucified with Christ, dead both to the law and to ourselves. But we are still united to Christ by faith.

LESSON 4

BY FAITH ALONE

Galatians 3:1–5

THE BIG PICTURE

For the first two chapters of Galatians, Paul has focused mainly on an autobiographical defense of his apostolic ministry, affirming his call from God, his acceptance by the other apostles, and even his authority to rebuke a fellow apostle when the implications of the gospel demand it! Now Paul turns with full force toward countering the false teaching that has somehow "bewitched" the Galatian believers (3:1). His words are far from gentle, and his point is clear: Christians who have begun their relationship with God through justification by faith alone must continue by faith alone. Justification by works has no role in the life of the Christian; it must not enter our lives and hearts, either before or after our conversion to Christ. After all, it is by faith in Jesus Christ that we receive the very Spirit of God (3:5)—so why would we want to turn to anything else as we seek to follow God?

Read Galatians 3:1–5.

GETTING STARTED

1. Think about a time when someone exposed—in your life—a wrong way of thinking, speaking, or acting. Assuming this was correct, how

did you initially *want* to respond? How did you *actually* respond? What was the result?

2. Give some examples of beginning something the right way, but then failing to continue in the right way. What might that look like in a job situation? What could that look like in a friendship or a marriage? Or on an athletic team?

OBSERVING THE TEXT

3. Take a moment and count the number of questions (in your English translation) that Paul asks the Galatians in this passage. How many did you find? Why do you think he asks all these questions?

Justification by Grace, pg. 80

This doctrine of justification by grace alone, through faith alone, in Christ alone has always had its detractors. If justification comes by grace, then all glory goes to God. But people want to keep some of the glory for themselves. Thus they seek to justify themselves before God by their own works.

4. How would you describe the general tone of this passage (note especially 3:1)? Why might Paul, at this point in the letter, be using this particular tone?

5. Begin to identify the main arguments that Paul is making in these verses. How is he exposing the dangers of some of the false teachings that the Galatians have heard?

UNDERSTANDING THE TEXT

6. Why do you think Paul uses the words "foolish" and "bewitched" in 3:1? What is he trying to communicate by using such strong language?

7. Why does Paul immediately call to the Galatians' minds to the crucifixion of Jesus (3:1), in response to the false teaching they are hearing? What is it about the cross that is so central to the teaching of justification by faith alone?

Adding to Christ's Work, pg. 85
Paul was upset with the Galatians because they were forgetting all of this. He had laid out for them Jesus Christ having been crucified. But then some other teachers had come along to write some graffiti on his billboard. Unwilling to accept salvation in Christ alone, they wanted to add their own finishing touches to the work of Christ.

8. Note Paul's repeated mention of "the Holy Spirit" (3:2, 5). Why is the Spirit so central to the way the Galatian Christians should think about their relationship with God? What is Paul saying about the Spirit in these verses, and how does the Spirit relate to salvation by faith?

9. Earlier we noted the rapid-fire questions that Paul asks the Galatian believers in this passage. What, specifically, is he asking them to consider in each of these questions? Consider them one by one, and summarize his various appeals.

10. How does Paul's teaching—that the Spirit comes through "hearing with faith"—impact the way we think about our lives as Christians? What are some implications of Paul's teaching for the way we think about the Holy Spirit working in our hearts and minds today?

BIBLE CONNECTIONS

11. The Galatian churches weren't the only churches experiencing the bewitching power of false gospels. They weren't even the only ones influenced by the teaching that one needs more than simply faith in Jesus to live a life that is pleasing to God. Take a moment and read Colossians 2:16–19. What false teachings seem to be influencing the Colossian church? How does Paul launch a counterattack against this teaching?

12. Long before Jesus came to earth, the Old Testament Scriptures were bearing witness to the fact that "hearing with faith" is what God truly desires from his people. Read Psalm 40:6–8. What does David, the psalmist, say is even more desirable to God than sacrifices and offerings? How might this truth relate to Galatians 3:1–5?

THEOLOGY CONNECTIONS

13. One of the historical champions of the doctrine of justification by faith alone is surely Martin Luther. He declared in 1528, in a sermon titled "On Faith and Coming to Christ": "This faith alone, when based upon the sure promises of God, must save us. . . . And in the light of it all, they must become fools who have taught us other ways to become godly." How does his language echo that of the apostle Paul's in Galatians

3:1–5? Why do you think Luther used such strong language ("fools"), especially in his historical context?

14. The Westminster Shorter Catechism defines sanctification, first, as "the work of God's free grace" (Q&A 35). Why is it so important to begin by defining sanctification in terms of what God does, even though we actively participate in our sanctification? How does this truth relate to the truths taught in Galatians 3:1–5?

APPLYING THE TEXT

15. What false teachings and influences do you think are most dangerous in potentially "bewitching" the church today? How can you be sure to identify those properly?

The Way In and the Way On, pg. 89
This truth—that the Holy Spirit comes by faith alone—has profound implications for the Christian life. It means that the Christian life finishes exactly the way it starts. The way *into* the Christian life is also the way *on in* the Christian life.

16. How can you remind yourself—and believers around you—to continue in the Christian life the same way we began the Christian life: by faith? What gets in the way of walking by faith, rather than by our works?

17. How can the doctrine of justification by faith, and faith alone, encourage those who are doubting their acceptance and goodness before God? How can this doctrine lift up those who are discouraged in their faith? How can this doctrine motivate joyful obedience?

PRAYER PROMPT

As you conclude your study of this passage, take some time to prayerfully search your own heart, and examine it for signs of self-justification. Ask God to fill you with faith, enabling you to trust the finished work of the crucified and risen Savior in your place. Pray that he would remind you that, by faith, you have the Holy Spirit indwelling you; rejoice, in Christ, that you need nothing else for justification or for sanctification!

LESSON 5

ABRAHAM'S FAMILY:
THE CURSE AND THE CROSS

Galatians 3:6–14

THE BIG PICTURE

For the first five verses of Galatians 3, Paul has been arguing primarily from experience, when it comes to the Galatians' consideration of their salvation by faith. "How did you come to know God in the first place, and how did you receive the Holy Spirit?" the apostle has been asking. Now, though, he will prove his point textually and biblically—from the Old Testament Scriptures that his Judaizing opponents prize so highly. Paul will go back to the life of their hero: Abraham. He will do this in order to prove that salvation is—and always has been—by faith alone, not by keeping the law. But he will go even further than this. Not only was Abraham justified by faith, apart from the law, but those who seek to become justified by keeping the law actually fall under a curse! No one is able to keep the law of God perfectly, and all humanity sits under the weight of God's condemnation because of sin. It is faith in Jesus Christ alone, who endured the curse of sin on the cross in our place, that will bring the blessing of God's salvation to all who put their faith in him—both Jews and Gentiles.

Read Galatians 3:6–14.

GETTING STARTED

1. Has there ever been a time when you sensed that you were excluded from a certain group or community? On what basis were you excluded? What was the effect of this experience on you, and how did you learn from it?

2. Have you ever had the experience of being openly and warmly accepted by a person or group in a way that you had not anticipated? What was the effect of that experience, and how did you learn from it?

OBSERVING THE TEXT

3. Begin by looking over the text carefully and observing the main human characters and groups that Paul mentions. Who are they? How many times does Paul mention them? What other parts of the Bible does Paul reference in these verses?

Abraham's Family, pg. 99
All who believe—and only those who believe—are children of Abraham. Membership in Abraham's family is not hereditary. Father Abraham's true sons and daughters are not the people who keep the law, but the people who live by faith. Their family resemblance is spiritual rather than physical.

4. If you were a Judaizer (and thus an opponent of Paul and his gospel), what would the tone of these verses feel like to you?

5. If you were a Gentile believer in the early church, how might this passage have a very different (and encouraging!) effect on you and your faith? Why?

UNDERSTANDING THE TEXT

6. Knowing what you already know about the Judaizers, why do you think that Paul would find it important and helpful to use Abraham as a reference point (3:6)? Why is referencing Abraham a powerful way to appeal to those who have been influenced by his Jewish opponents?

7. Paul makes a massive statement in Galatians 3:8: "God . . . preached the gospel beforehand to Abraham." What statement from God to Abraham is Paul referring to here? How is this indeed a proclamation of the gospel of Jesus Christ, long before Jesus came to earth (see Gen. 12:1–3)?

8. Why does Paul quote from Deuteronomy 27:26 in Galatians 3:10? What point is he making about human sin? What point is he making about the law? How does this point push back against the teaching of the Judaizers?

9. What point is Paul making in verses 11–12 about living by faith, rather than living by the law? How do these verses relate to what Paul has just said in verse 10? Why is the phrase from Habakkuk such a significant one for Paul (v. 11)?

10. How does Paul explain in verse 13 what Jesus Christ did on the cross for us? Why do the effects of Jesus' death apply to both Jews and Gentiles who have faith, according to Paul? Why is this point so important, given the context of the Galatian believers? What, specifically, do the Gentiles receive through faith, and why is Paul careful to note this?

The Law's Curse, pg. 109

If it is true that everyone, without exception, is condemned by the curse of the law, then why would anyone ever try to base salvation on keeping the law? This is Paul's point. Everyone who depends on the law is under a curse because the law curses everyone who breaks it, which everyone does. Ironically, by advocating obedience to the law the Judaizers were not escaping God's curse but actually incurring it!

BIBLE CONNECTIONS

11. Since the book of Genesis plays such a big role in this passage from Galatians, take a moment to read Genesis 12:1–3 and then Genesis 15:1–6. Why are God's promises to Abraham in Genesis 12 so massive and ultimately Christ-centered? Why does Genesis 15:6 come to be such an important verse for Paul in thinking about justification by faith alone?

12. The New Testament gospels record Jesus, from the cross, quoting in anguish the first verse of Psalm 22: "My God, my God, why have you forsaken me?" How does Galatians 3:10–14 help you to better understand that cry of Jesus from the cross?

THEOLOGY CONNECTIONS

13. In the Westminster Confession of Faith, saving faith is described with these words: "By this faith, a Christian believeth to be true whatsoever is revealed in the Word, for the authority of God Himself speaking therein; and acteth differently upon that which each particular passage thereof containeth; yielding obedience to the commands, trembling at the threatenings, and embracing the promises of God for this life, and that which is to come. But the principal acts of saving faith are accepting, receiving, and resting upon Christ alone for justification, sanctification, and eternal life, by virtue of the covenant of grace" (14.2). How do these words beautifully describe the faith of Abraham, which Paul

holds up as the ideal example in our passage? How can these words help you to better understand your own faith in Christ?

14. The Westminster Shorter Catechism asks: "What doth every sin deserve?" The answer given is: "Every sin deserveth God's wrath and curse, both in this life, and that which is to come" (Q&A 84). How does this brief question and answer expand your view of your sin and guilt before God? How does it help you to better understand the wonder of Jesus Christ bearing the wrath of God against your sin on the cross?

APPLYING THE TEXT

15. Paul emphasizes that the blessing of Abraham (salvation) comes to the Gentiles "through faith" (v. 14). What does this mean for our engagement in evangelism? How can this passage spur you on toward even more involvement in the spreading of the gospel of Jesus Christ to all peoples?

16. How does Paul's language of the "curse" of the law and the "curse" that fell upon Jesus on the cross for our redemption (v. 13) expand your

understanding of both your sin and God's grace? What is the right response to this kind of grace, and how can you respond more properly to it?

17. How are you tempted to veer away from living by faith, and instead to live by your own strength and will? In what ways do you need to return to the centrality of the cross of Jesus Christ and its significance in your ongoing walk with the Lord?

PRAYER PROMPT

As you close this time of study in Galatians 3:6–14, pray that God would assure you in a fresh way of your inclusion in his family—the family of Abraham—through faith in his Son. Ask God to remind you of the curse of your sin, as well as your utter failure to obey him and keep his law perfectly. But pray that you would trust Jesus more deeply, knowing that he bore the curse for you, so that God's blessing and Spirit might come to you.

The Cross and the Curse, pgs. 117–18

In that old cursed cross we see the wrath of God against the sin of humanity. The cross is a public demonstration for all time of his condemnation. Having seen the God-man on the cursed tree, who can doubt the sinfulness of sin or the wrath of God? Yet in the same cursed cross we see more clearly than anywhere else the power of divine grace.

LESSON 6

THE LAW AND THE
PROMISE OF CHRIST

Galatians 3:15–29

THE BIG PICTURE

For the final fifteen verses of Galatians 3, Paul's focus is on the law of God and its connection to the grace and salvation of God's people in Christ. Previously, he has argued both from experience and from the Old Testament that salvation comes by faith alone, apart from works of the law. God's people are not justified by obedience to the law, but through the finished work of Jesus, who took our curse for sin on the cross in our place. Now, though, Paul takes time to explain the place of the law and the graciousness of God in giving it to his people. The law does not nullify the promise of God fulfilled in Christ, which Abraham received by faith 430 years before the law was ever given! But the law was a good gift of God—a "guardian" for his people because of sin. It is Jesus Christ who, through his death on the cross, frees all of those held captive by the law (and condemned by it), and invites all people of faith into the family of God.

Read Galatians 3:15–29.

55

GETTING STARTED

1. Have you ever had the experience of thinking that something—a certain part, tool, or test—was superfluous or unnecessary, only to realize later how important it actually was? Please explain why.

2. What are some questions you have had in the past, or have currently, about the Old Testament law of God? Have you ever wondered what the purpose of the law really was? Describe some ways that you may have questioned the ongoing importance of a particular law or wondered what role it should serve in your life as a Christian.

OBSERVING THE TEXT

3. Take a moment and note all the different things that Paul says about the law in this passage. What reasons does he provide for the giving of the law? What metaphors does he use to describe the law and its role in the lives of God's people?

Abraham's Salvation, pg. 127

When God gave Moses the law, Abraham had been dead for centuries. Fortunately, he had been justified by faith long before the law of Moses was even introduced. Abraham's salvation was not based on anything Abraham did. The covenant did not establish any legal requirements that he had to satisfy. It all came free, the way an inheritance always does.

4. Why, in the course of this letter, might Paul now feel the need to explain the proper place for the law, as well as its usefulness? What points has he made earlier about the law that might lead one to think that it was almost a bad thing?

5. Examine Paul's use of questions in this passage. What questions does he ask? How does he answer them? In what ways are the concluding verses of the passage (vv. 26–29) delivered in a slightly different tone and with a different intention?

UNDERSTANDING THE TEXT

6. What "human example" is Paul using, in 3:15–18, to illustrate his point about the preeminence of faith in the promise of God to Abraham and his spiritual family? How is this metaphor helpful in understanding God's covenant with his people—down through the centuries?

7. Notice that Paul places much emphasis on the singularity of Abraham's "offspring" (that is, "seed," referring to Christ) in verse 16. What is Paul teaching about the promise of God to Abraham in this verse? If God's

promise really does connect to the ultimate coming of Christ, why would that promise remain unchanged by the law?

8. What does Paul mean when he says that the law was "added because of transgressions" (v. 19)? How might Romans 5:20 and 7:7 illuminate the meaning of this phrase? How does the Old Testament law expose sin in ways that would not have been possible without it?

9. How do Paul's pictures of the law in Galatians 3:23–25, as a prison and a guardian, help us to understand the purpose of God's law more clearly? What is he seeking to teach about the law by using these metaphors? How is the familial language of verses 26–30 meant to stand in stark contrast to these pictures of the law?

The Law and Death, pg. 136

The law is something like chemotherapy. When chemotherapy is used to treat cancer, it does not give life. Actually, it is an instrument of death. The chemicals that are poured into the body destroy healthy tissue as well as cancer cells. During the course of treatment, chemotherapy actually makes the patient feel much worse. But it is all necessary for the patient's long-term health. In much the same way, the law makes us worse so that Christ can make us better.

10. Note Paul's description of an abolition of distinctions, in Christ, for all who are "sons of God, through faith" (3:26). What does this teach us about God's character? What kind of unity do believers in Jesus share with one another? Does this unity mean that personal distinctions (ethnic, social, gender) cease to exist? If not, then what does Paul mean?

BIBLE CONNECTIONS

11. Paul describes the struggle of the law, and its capacity to identify and even increase human sin, in his well-known words of Romans 7. Turn there now and read verses 7–13. What parallels do you observe between that passage and this one from Galatians 3? What does Paul say in Romans 7 that adds to what he says in this passage from Galatians?

12. Read 1 Peter 2:9–10. What do you notice about the way that Peter describes the identity of the ethnically mixed (Jew and Gentile) churches of ancient Asia Minor? How is Peter speaking truths about the wonderful, unified family of God that are similar to those spoken by Paul?

THEOLOGY CONNECTIONS

13. One of the metaphors that Paul uses for the law in this passage is that of a "guardian," indicating that the law watched over God's people until the coming of Christ. The Heidelberg Catechism asks, "From where do you know your sins and misery?" The answer is: "From the law of God" (Q&A 3). How might the law have "guarded" the people of God by showing them their sin and their need for God's grace? Why would the law's revealing of their sin and misery have been a gracious gift from God for those who looked to him in faith?

14. Galatians 3 closes with a beautiful reminder of our adoption, by faith, as true children of God. Here is how the Westminster Confession of Faith describes adoption: "All those that are justified, God vouchsafeth, in and for His only Son Jesus Christ, to make partakers of the grace of adoption, by which they are taken into the number, and enjoy the liberties and privileges of the children of God, have His name put upon them, receive the spirit of adoption, have access to the throne of grace with boldness, are enabled to cry, Abba, Father, are pitied, protected, provided for, and chastened by Him as by a Father: yet never cast off, but sealed to the day of redemption; and inherit the promises, as heirs of everlasting salvation" (chapter 12). How does this description expand your view of God's love for you as his child?

APPLYING THE TEXT

15. If our salvation ultimately rests on the promise of God, which he can never break, what should that mean for the way we live? How should

the security of God's promise form our attitude toward God? How should that shape the way we obey the commands of God?

16. In what life situations are you most tempted to doubt your status as a son or daughter of God, through faith in Christ? What emotions lead you toward this kind of doubt? How can the truths of this passage encourage your faith, hope, and joy as a child of God in the days ahead?

17. In what ways do you, or people around you, tend to revert to making distinctions between groups of Christians? How have you seen this happen with regard to gender? Ethnicity? Social class? What practical steps could you take toward unity with someone you are tempted to marginalize or exclude, based on what Paul teaches in Galatians 3:28?

Distinctions and Unity, pg. 153

Being in Christ establishes a fundamental unity within which our diversity can be cherished. Ethnic distinctions remain. Paul did not cease to be a Jew when he became a Christian, but continued to value his ethnic heritage. . . . Our ethnic, social, and sexual distinctions continue to exist. But since we are in Christ, these distinctions do not divide us. They do not determine our standing in God's family.

PRAYER PROMPT

As you close your study of this dense and difficult passage about the law of God, spend some time praising God for his good and gracious gift of the law, given to his people. Thank him for the gift of graciously exposing sin and showing us the need for a Savior. Give him praise that, because of the work of Jesus Christ on the cross, we can now be sons and daughters of God—no longer under a guardian, but part of his true family of faith.

LESSON 7

FROM SLAVERY TO SONSHIP

Galatians 4:1–7

THE BIG PICTURE

As you know from our study of the concluding verses of Galatians 3, Paul makes use of some helpful metaphors to describe the function of the Old Testament law in the lives of God's people in the days before the coming of Christ. The law was, in certain respects, like a prison—holding God's people and identifying their sin in anticipation of the freedom and forgiveness of the gospel. The law was also like a guardian, keeping close watch on Israel until the reality of being children of God was fully realized through Jesus' death and resurrection. Now Paul moves on to another analogy: life under the law is like life as an "heir" to a great inheritance. A son who anticipates a large inheritance has, for a while, little more freedom than a slave; the promised riches are his right, but he does not yet possess them as he lives under strict guidance and discipline. But with the coming of Jesus Christ in God's good timing, the heirs living under the law come into the full possession of the very Spirit of God. All of God's people who put their faith in Jesus now know the joy of full acceptance and spiritual riches as his sons and daughters, as well as the intimacy of being able to call God "Abba, Father" (4:6).

Read Galatians 4:1–7.

GETTING STARTED

1. Describe a time when someone challenged you to "Grow up!" Or perhaps there came a time when you saw your need to develop more maturity in a certain area. What led you to realize the need for growing up or developing maturity? What was the result?

2. What are some of the challenges that come with both freedom and responsibility? What are some of the joys and benefits that come with them, in specific life situations you have experienced?

OBSERVING THE TEXT

3. What is the main analogy that runs throughout this passage? Why is this a helpful and vivid one? What aspects of Paul's historical context (inheritance law in the Roman world, etc.) might help you better understand the analogy he is using in these verses?

4. How does Paul's use of contrast play a large part in what he is communicating in Galatians 4:1–7? What two positions or stations is he

contrasting? What are the benefits of one and the limitations of the other?

5. What repeated words and phrases do you notice in these verses? What does Paul seem to be emphasizing the most? To what ideas does he call the Galatians' attention most earnestly?

UNDERSTANDING THE TEXT

6. What do you suppose Paul means by his use of the phrase "elementary principles of the world" (4:3)? In what ways does the Old Testament law of God connect with—and reinforce—the basic principles of our world? Why is this connection quite logical and sensible, given God's role as Creator?

Children and Slaves, pg. 159

Whether the term "elementary principles" refers to God's law for the Jews (which seems more probable) or to Satan's control of the Gentiles, the point is that eventually God's people needed to grow up. For a time, they were no better off than slaves. Indeed, while they were children, they practically had to be treated as slaves. But in truth they had always been sons, so the day finally came when they left their religious infancy behind and grew into full spiritual maturity.

7. What is Paul emphasizing to the Galatians by repeating the phrase "under the law" in verses 4–5? What does it mean that Jesus was born "under the law" (v. 4), and why is that important? How does that reality relate to Jesus' redemption of those who are "under the law" (v. 5)?

8. In just a few short words in Galatians 4:4–5, what important truths does Paul teach about both the coming and the identity of Jesus Christ? How does the word "redeem" explain the significance of Jesus' death on the cross for those who are under the law? How do all of these truths about Jesus connect to our "adoption" as sons and daughters of God (v. 5)?

Slavery to Sonship, pg. 164

Now everyone who believes in the risen Christ is God's own dear child. If we continue to serve God out of fear or duty, however, we show that we do not understand what Christ has done on our behalf. Christianity is not a bondage, but a freedom, for Christ has brought us from slavery into sonship. Our ongoing membership in God's family does not depend on our works, as if somehow we had to earn our keep.

9. What effect does God's sending of "the Spirit of his Son into our hearts" have on our interaction with God the Father (v. 6)? When we address the Father as "Abba," what significance does that have? Why should this intimacy with the Creator God be astounding to us, but also deeply encouraging?

10. How does Galatians 4:7 serve as a succinct and clear conclusion to this passage? What points does Paul reiterate? Of what truths does he remind the Galatian believers one final time?

BIBLE CONNECTIONS

11. Psalm 119, the longest psalm in the Bible, is a beautiful "love song" about the law of God. Read the final verse of this psalm—Psalm 119:176. What is the significance of the way this psalm ends? What does its conclusion suggest about the insufficiency of the law and the slavery that must be broken by Christ alone?

12. Take a moment to read Romans 8:14–17, a passage in which Paul speaks in similar ways to Galatians 4:7 about the Spirit of God and our adoption as sons. How does Paul, in the Romans passage, say that we can be sure of our adoption by God?

THEOLOGY CONNECTIONS

13. The Westminster Confession of Faith says this about the ceremonial law of the Old Testament: "Besides this law, commonly called moral, God was pleased to give to the people of Israel, as a church under age, ceremonial laws, containing several typical ordinances, partly of worship, prefiguring Christ, His graces, actions, sufferings, and benefits; and partly, holding forth divers instructions of moral duties. All which ceremonial laws are now abrogated, under the new testament" (19.3). What does the Westminster Confession of Faith teach about the connection between the ceremonial law and Jesus Christ? How does this relate to the move from slavery to sonship, as described by Paul in Galatians 4:1–7?

14. The great Reformer John Calvin wrote: "With what confidence would anyone address God as 'Father'? Who would break forth into such rashness as to claim for himself the honor of a son of God unless we had been adopted as children of grace in Christ? He, while he is the true Son, has of himself been given us as a brother that what he has of his own by nature may become ours by benefit of adoption if we embrace this great blessing with sure faith" (*Institutes*, 3.20.36). How

does Calvin expand on the ideas in this passage in Galatians? What is particularly encouraging to you from this quotation?

APPLYING THE TEXT

15. What truths about the coming, identity, and work of Jesus Christ do you struggle most to believe? How can you remind yourself daily of Christ's redemptive work for you, as well as your resulting adoption into the family of God?

16. What might be some hints or signs that you are behaving as God's slave, rather than as his child? How can you more fully live, think, and speak as an adopted child of God, rather than out of a spirit of slavery and fear?

The Spirit's Whisper, pg. 167
First God sent his Son to save us from our sins and to make us all his sons and daughters. The Son is the elder brother who picks us up and sets us down on God's lap. Then, God sent his Holy Spirit—the Divine Whisper—who tells us that we will always be God's special children. When we hear the Spirit's whisper, our hearts cry out to God, "You will always be my Father."

17. What attitudes, behaviors, or spiritual habits prevent you from addressing God intimately as "Abba, Father" (4:6)?

PRAYER PROMPT

Galatians 4:1–7 lays out a beautiful, Trinitarian picture that should inform all of our prayers as Christians! Through the redemptive work of God the Son, God the Spirit enables our new hearts to pray lovingly and worshipfully to God the Father, who promises to accept us as his true children. Pray, today, with thankfulness for this cosmic adoption that has taken place through the work of our gracious God!

LESSON 8

A PLEA FROM A
PERPLEXED PASTOR

Galatians 4:8–20

THE BIG PICTURE

Up to this point in Paul's letter to the Galatians, we have seen several glimpses of the apostle's emotional involvement in their spiritual well-being. He has already used some strong language in denouncing the harmful teachings of the Judaizers and calling the Galatian believers back to faith in Christ alone as the key to their salvation and their ongoing walk with God as adopted children. But in Galatians 4:8–20, the personal nature of Paul's appeal becomes most pointed. He has been in teaching mode—using metaphors, analogies, and arguments from the Old Testament to argue against slavery to the law and in favor of faith-filled freedom in Christ. Now Paul will make an earnest and emotional appeal to the Galatians on the basis of their personal relationship. Paul pleads with them not to abandon the gospel and return to slavery under the law. He tells them that he thinks of them as his own "children" (4:19), anguishing over them as a parent does over a lost child. In short, here is a pastor who is utterly perplexed by his people—people who have believed the gospel, but are now in danger of turning away from it.

Read Galatians 4:8–20.

71

GETTING STARTED

1. Describe a time when someone made an appeal to you on the basis of his or her relationship with you. Perhaps it was a parent, a friend, or even a spouse, asking you to act or respond in a certain way because of the relationship. Why was the personal nature of the appeal so powerful? What effect did the appeal have on you?

2. Think of some of the most impassioned pleas that *you* have made to people in your life. How did you try to make your point? What emotions did you have as you made your pleas? What kind of response were you hoping for?

OBSERVING THE TEXT

3. What seems to be the general tone of this passage? What words and phrases contribute to this tone? Describe your sense of Paul's emotions as he writes Galatians 4:8–20.

Squandering the Inheritance, pg. 169

By the Spirit of God's Son, the Galatians had learned to call God "Father." Yet they were in imminent danger of going from sonship right back into slavery. They were about to squander their spiritual inheritance by selling their birthright as the sons and daughters of God.

4. What phrases and ideas from earlier in the letter does Paul reference in this passage? How is this appeal a further development of points he has made in earlier chapters?

5. How does Paul contrast his ministry and his love for the Galatian believers with the influence of his enemies (the Judaizers)? How does he describe his feelings toward the members of the church? What does he say about the behavior and motivation of his opponents?

UNDERSTANDING THE TEXT

6. Where has Paul used the phrase "elementary principles of the world" before? What further hints do you get about what he means by the phrase here in chapter 4? In what ways are the Galatian believers in great danger of becoming "enslaved" again by these principles?

7. According to Galatians 4:8–11, what are some implicit signs that a person has truly grasped the gospel of grace and is living by it? What might be some explicit signs that a person has fallen back into a "slave" mentality with regard to religion? What does this slave mentality look

like in the Galatian context, based on the words Paul uses in these verses?

8. Read Galatians 4:12–16 again. Describe the Galatians' original response to Paul's preaching of the gospel. How does Paul remember them responding to the gospel and his preaching? What phrases does he use to describe their devotion to him and his gospel? How does he imply that they are changing their response, both to him and to his gospel message?

9. What are some ways in which Paul contrasts his ministry to the Galatians (and his motives in ministry to them) with that of his opponents (4:17–20)? What are his goals for them as he serves them in gospel ministry? What do the Judaizers seem to be after?

Rejecting the Gospel, pg. 175
Paul writes to the Galatians, therefore, as a wounded lover. . . . His gospel has not changed. He is still proclaiming the good news about the cross and the empty tomb. He is still preaching justification by grace alone, through faith alone, in Christ alone. Yet the Galatians were starting to reject the one true gospel. Unwilling to hear the truth, they were treating Paul like an enemy.

10. Based on verses 17–20, why do you think the Judaizers might have succeeded in winning some of the Galatian believers to their teaching, or at least significantly influencing them?

BIBLE CONNECTIONS

11. Throughout redemptive history, God has graciously provided servant leaders for his people, who love them and are after their ultimate good as they believe and obey God. Take a moment and read Moses' impassioned plea to God on behalf of the Israelites in Exodus 32:30–32. How is Moses' heart for God's people similar to Paul's heart for the Galatian believers?

12. Jesus, too, is passionately committed to his people holding on to the gospel of grace. In Revelation 3:14–22, read Jesus' strong rebuke to the church of Laodicea. What core teaching does this church seem to have abandoned? How does Jesus make an emotional and dramatic appeal that is similar to Paul's appeal in Galatians?

THEOLOGY CONNECTIONS

13. The Westminster Confession of Faith, on the topic of Christian liberty, says this: "God alone is Lord of the conscience, and hath left it

free from the doctrines and commandments of men, which are, in any thing, contrary to His Word; or beside it, if matters of faith, or worship. So that, to believe such doctrines, or to obey such commands, out of conscience, is to betray true liberty of conscience: and the requiring of an implicit faith, and an absolute and blind obedience, is to destroy liberty of conscience, and reason also" (20.2). How does this statement speak to the importance of the freedom we have through faith in Christ Jesus? What connections do you see between this statement and Paul's stern warnings in Galatians 4:8–20?

14. The Heidelberg Catechism describes true saving faith as "a firm confidence that not only to others, but also to me, God has granted forgiveness of sins, everlasting righteousness, and salvation, out of mere grace" (Q&A 21). How do the Galatians, according to 4:8–20, seem to be in danger of abandoning this kind of faith? What is at risk when Christians are tempted to abandon such faith?

APPLYING THE TEXT

15. It is perplexing to Paul that the Galatians, who once received gospel preaching with joy, are now wandering away from it. What forces and winds of our culture today might lead you to abandon the joyful

acceptance of the gospel of grace? What tendencies can creep into the church and damage the doctrine of salvation by faith alone?

16. How can you be vigilant to continue receiving the Word of God with joy, rather than growing cold toward it and eventually growing hungry for some other teaching?

17. In the light of Paul's description of his ministry to the Galatian believers (4:17–20) and his humble commitment to them, how can you grow in your evangelistic and discipleship commitment to those around you in a way that follows the pattern of Paul? How can you draw near to people in your community who do not know Christ, in order that they may draw near to Christ as well?

Knowing the Context, pg. 177

[Paul] knew how to become so integrated into the life of a community that he could explain the gospel in words that people could actually understand. This is the strategy Paul followed when he first visited the Galatians. He entered into their lives so thoroughly that he practically became a Galatian himself.

PRAYER PROMPT

As you close your study of Galatians 4:8–20, look back on your initial reception of, and belief in, the gospel of Jesus Christ. Ask God to fill you with renewed joy as you consider the hope of sins forgiven, eternal life with God, and the gift of the indwelling Holy Spirit—all yours through faith in Jesus Christ. Pray that God would give you strength to hold on to his pure gospel, never turning aside to any teaching or way of thinking that would do damage to its power in your life.

LESSON 9

TWO MOTHERS, TWO SONS, TWO COVENANTS

Galatians 4:21–31

THE BIG PICTURE

As we have seen in our study of the book of Galatians, Paul finds it necessary to go back to the Old Testament Scriptures in order to prove the veracity and sufficiency of the gospel of grace and faith that he preaches. After all, these are the very Scriptures that his opponents, the Judaizers, claim to believe and obey! In Galatians 4:21–31, Paul goes back to the Old Testament yet again, this time to make what he calls an "allegorical" argument from the account of Abraham's two sons, Isaac and Ishmael. To one son, Ishmael, he connects the Judaizers: they, like Ishmael, are children of slavery and not born of the "promise" of God. To the other son, Isaac, he connects the family of faith, who live according to the promise of God. All children of God are children of freedom, who enter God's family miraculously by faith because of God's immense grace through Jesus Christ. True faith is likened to the miraculous birth given by God to Isaac—not like the ordinary birth of Ishmael that was the product of Abraham's relationship with his wife's servant.

Read Galatians 4:21–31.

GETTING STARTED

1. Have you ever heard someone start a sentence by saying, "There are only two kinds of people in this world . . ."? Give some examples that you have heard, including any that are humorous!

2. Why is it so important to people that they know their heritage and where they came from? What do you think lies behind the current fascination with genealogies and ancestral lines? Why might it be more important to know our spiritual heritage and ancestry than our biological background?

OBSERVING THE TEXT

3. Notice Paul's use of questions throughout this passage. What specific questions does he ask the Galatians? What points is he trying to make? In what ways does he challenge their thinking?

Ishmael and Isaac, pg. 184

From the very beginning there was a fundamental spiritual difference between the two sons. One son was born by proxy, the other by promise. One came by works; the other came by faith. One was a slave; the other was free. Thus Ishmael and Isaac represent two entirely different approaches to religion: law against grace, flesh against Spirit, self-reliance against divine dependence.

4. This entire passage hinges on Paul looking back to the Old Testament. Where does he take the Galatians in Jewish history? Why do you think he chooses to reference these stories and passages?

5. What is meant to be comforting and encouraging to the Galatian believers in this passage? How has Paul's tone changed a bit from Galatians 4:8–20, the passage you studied in the previous chapter?

UNDERSTANDING THE TEXT

6. Read Galatians 4:23 again. In what way was Ishmael "born according to the flesh" (see Gen. 16:1–3)? What about Isaac's birth makes Paul say that he was "born through promise"? What distinctions is Paul drawing between these two sons, based on the narrative from the book of Genesis?

The Spiritual Jerusalem, pg. 187
The New Jerusalem is not just for the future. God has already started to build his eternal city. The "new" Jerusalem has replaced the "now" Jerusalem. The spiritual Jerusalem has superseded the earthly Jerusalem in the plan of God. The promises of the Old Testament were not for the Jews only, but they are fulfilled in the church of Jesus Christ.

7. How, according to Paul, is Hagar representative of the old covenant and those living under slavery to the law (Gal. 4:24–25)? In what ways does Paul allegorically connect her to this entire religious system? How and why does Sarah represent, for Paul, the new covenant of grace, and not Jerusalem and the law?

8. Why would it have been surprising to the Judaizers to hear Paul identify them as children of Hagar, not of Sarah? How would the Judaizers have thought of themselves? Why might Galatians 4:25 have been particularly shocking, and even offensive, to Paul's Jewish opponents?

9. What point is Paul making by quoting Isaiah 54:1 in Galatians 4:27? How is he using this passage to explain the reality of living as children of Sarah—free children of the promise?

10. Explain why, given the Galatians' context, Paul mentions the persecution of Isaac and Sarah by Ishmael and Hagar. Why might he have made that connection? What is the ultimate hope offered by Paul to the children of promise, who live in the freedom of the gospel (4:30)?

BIBLE CONNECTIONS

11. Obviously, Galatians 4:21–31 takes us to the portion of the Old Testament that describes the story of Ishmael and Isaac—the two sons of Abraham. Take a moment to read Genesis 16:1–6. What do Abraham's actions in this account reveal about his attitude toward the promise of God that his wife would bear him a son? What is the result of his actions with Hagar in the immediate context?

12. The other Old Testament passage referenced by Paul in this passage is Isaiah 54:1; he quotes it word for word. Read Isaiah 54:1–5. What promise is revealed in these verses? How does it relate to the overall message of the book of Galatians?

THEOLOGY CONNECTIONS

13. The Westminster Confession of Faith says about the law of God: "This law, after his fall, continued to be a perfect rule of righteousness; and, as such, was delivered by God upon Mount Sinai, in ten commandments" (19.2). How is it possible for the law of God to be "a perfect rule of righteousness" given on Mount Sinai, but for the apostle Paul to also identify Mount Sinai with Hagar and the children of slavery? What have you learned so far in your study of Galatians that enables you to put these two truths together?

14. John Wycliffe, an early Reformer who faced intense persecution because of his commitment to translating the Word of God into the language of the people, once remarked: "The Gospel alone is sufficient to rule the lives of Christians everywhere; any additional rules made to govern men's conduct added nothing to the perfection already found in the Gospel of Jesus Christ." How do Wycliffe's words relate to Paul's argument in the book of Galatians? In what ways could "additional rules," when added to the gospel, put one firmly in the family of Hagar, rather than the family of promise?

APPLYING THE TEXT

15. We have seen that Abraham's approach to the birth of Ishmael and his approach to the birth of Isaac can represent two different ways of relating to God. One way is by human effort and law; the other is through God's grace and faith. How can you tell when you are beginning to live by human effort and law, rather than by God's grace and faith? What warning signs might you identify in your thoughts, attitudes, and worship?

16. To be a child of God—a citizen of the "Jerusalem above" (4:26)—is the greatest honor and privilege in the world! What causes you to forget this? What happens in the rhythms of your daily life that makes you most prone to wander from the joy and peace that come from knowing your true identity in Christ?

17. What can you learn from the acknowledgment of persecution that Paul gives to the Galatians in 4:29? How can you prepare your mind and your heart for the struggles and trials that will come as you live as a child of the promise? In what ways can you remind yourself—and others—of the final hope offered by Paul for the free children of grace?

PRAYER PROMPT

In his pursuit of an heir apart from the promise of God, Abraham took matters into his own hands rather than trusting God's gracious work in God's time. In your time of prayer following your study of this passage, confess your tendency to act like a child of slavery, rather than a child of promise. Ask God to remind you of the miraculous birth into the new Jerusalem that you have received by faith in Christ alone. Pray that he would give you grace to live as a child of the "free woman" and as part of the Jerusalem above.

Real Christians Suffer, pg. 190

Persecution is one way to tell the difference between true and false religion. Persecution is the opposition Christians face for speaking or doing God's will. It can include ridicule, loss, violence, and even martyrdom. One of the distinguishing marks of real Christians is that they are willing to suffer persecution for their faith, and even to die for it.

LESSON 10

FAITH AND FREEDOM

Galatians 5:1–12

THE BIG PICTURE

Many scholars and commentators have pointed out that Galatians 5 seems to begin a new section in Paul's letter. He has written *autobiographically* (chapters 1–2), then *theologically* (chapters 3–4), and now *ethically*. To put it in different words, chapters 5 and 6 of Galatians move toward more practical and moral instructions about how the Galatian Christians should live out their faith, relying on God's grace in every situation and detail of their spiritual lives. Specifically, the practice of circumcision is very much on Paul's mind in this passage; we can assume that at least one aspect of the Judaizers' message was that uncircumcised Christians had to be circumcised, in accordance with Old Testament law, in order to become full-fledged followers of God. Paul vehemently rejects this teaching, arguing that submission to circumcision as a requirement for favor with God actually would risk the entire reality of salvation by grace alone through faith alone! He exhorts the Galatian believers almost like a concerned parent, urging them to stick close to the message of the cross that he preached to them, rather than being hindered by the Judaizers. He reserves some of his strongest and most ferocious language for those who would keep the Galatians from their freedom and fullness in Christ.

Read Galatians 5:1–12.

GETTING STARTED

1. Have you ever had to jump through unnecessary hoops in order to make a purchase, join a group, or begin a project? Describe the frustrations that can come when unnecessary steps are added to a process that should be quite simple. How might this experience relate to that of the Galatian believers, who were being assaulted by the Judaizers?

2. Discuss the concept of freedom. What are some of the different ways in which people in our world today define freedom? How does the Bible, in your view, define freedom? What is problematic about some of the definitions of freedom that people put forward?

OBSERVING THE TEXT

3. Look again at Galatians 5:1–12 and note the repeated words and phrases. How often does Paul mention circumcision? Why might that be? How often does Paul mention freedom? Why might that be?

True Freedom, pg. 194

True freedom, therefore, is not self-fulfillment. It is not merely political independence or social equality. It is not the kind of liberty that leads to license, the freedom to do whatever we want or believe whatever we choose. True freedom means liberation from sin, death, and the devil. And by the grace of God, this is exactly the kind of liberation Christ has come to provide.

4. Where in this passage does Paul use the strongest language? To whom is this language directed? What does the intensity of Paul's writing at certain points in Galatians tell you about what he values the most?

5. What two different groups of people does Paul deal with in Galatians 5:1–12? How would you describe his attitude and tone toward them?

UNDERSTANDING THE TEXT

6. In Galatians 5:1 (which functions as a thesis statement for this passage), how does Paul summarize his ethical call to the Galatian believers? Why is "freedom" such an important word for him to use? What does Paul mean by "freedom" (5:1)?

7. In verses 2–4, Paul seems to imply that even simply accepting the Judaizers' call to circumcision to gain acceptance with God endangers one's entire walk with God by faith and through grace alone. Why is that teaching so dangerous? Why would the embrace of circumcision obligate the Galatians to keep "the whole law" (v. 3)? Why would giving in to this pressure from the Judaizers "sever" them from Christ (v. 4)?

8. Why would Paul's minimizing of circumcision (v. 6) be offensive and shocking to many Jewish believers? What is the one crucial thing in the lives of believers in Jesus (vv. 5–6)?

9. How does Paul describe the influence of the Judaizers in verses 7–9? What metaphors does he use for his opponents and their teaching? How does Paul make use of probing questions in his warnings to the Galatians?

10. What does Paul say will become of the Judaizers and their message (5:10)? What does Paul affirm about his own ministry and message, and the consistent focus of his teaching and preaching? Why is the cross offensive, and why must that be the main thing that offends as the gospel is preached (v. 11)? What should we think of Paul's intense exclamation in verse 12?

Real Faith and Works, pg. 204
The last thing Paul says about justifying faith is that it actually works. The only kind of faith that is worth anything is the kind of faith that expresses itself through love. This does not mean that we are justified by love . . . [but] the faith that alone justifies is never alone. True faith is always a working faith, a faith that works.

BIBLE CONNECTIONS

11. Read Genesis 17:1–14. Obviously, circumcision was a big deal to God's people for centuries and centuries. What was this sacred rite meant to indicate? Why would it have been so difficult for some Jewish Christians to give up circumcision as a requirement for every male follower of God?

12. Now read Colossians 2:11–14. How does this passage help us to understand what circumcision was always meant to symbolize for the people of God? Explain how you, as a first-century Gentile Christian, might have used these verses to express your fullness and completeness in Christ following your repentance of sin and faith in him.

THEOLOGY CONNECTIONS

13. Question 85 of the Westminster Shorter Catechism asks what God requires of us, that we may escape his wrath and curse due to us for our sin. The answer: "To escape the wrath and curse of God due to us for sin, God requireth of us faith in Jesus Christ, repentance unto life, with the diligent use of all the outward means whereby Christ communicateth to us the benefits of redemption." Why is it such an affront to God to add anything to what he has required of us for our salvation

(namely, faith in his Son)? How does this affront help you understand Paul's passion and anger in Galatians 5:1–12?

14. The Swiss Reformer Huldrych Zwingli once wrote: "Our confidence in Christ does not make us lazy, negligent, or careless, but on the contrary it awakens us, urges us on, and makes us active in living righteous lives and doing good. There is no self-confidence to compare with this." How does this statement articulate well the true meaning of Christian freedom, to which Paul calls the Galatians in the passage you have studied?

APPLYING THE TEXT

15. Most likely, you are not being tempted daily to live according to all of the regulations of the Old Testament law! But how might you be drawn toward an "earning favor" mentality in your walk with God? In what ways do you feel most prone to wander away from the freedom that God has given you through faith in Jesus, into a soul-destroying legalism instead?

16. While it may be prudent not to repeat Paul's exact language in Galatians 5:12, what does his passion and anger teach us about how to respond to teaching that undermines the gospel? How have you been guilty of

not speaking strongly enough against messages from your culture or community that oppose the gospel of salvation by Christ alone and by grace alone?

17. How have you been guilty of offending friends and acquaintances with something other than the message of the cross of Jesus Christ? What makes you prone to avoid offending others by not speaking about the gospel? How can you grow in both of those areas?

PRAYER PROMPT

Paul reserves some of his strongest language in the entire letter for those who would infect the gospel of grace with a demand to do something more than what Christ has done to gain favor with God. Pray that God would allow you to trust more deeply today in the finished work of Jesus Christ for you on the cross. Pray also that you would proclaim the message of the cross, even if it brings offense and contempt your way.

The Exclusivity of Christ, pg. 215

Christ crucified—more than anything else, this is why Christianity is so offensive to a postmodern culture. Most people think well of Jesus Christ, as least as a moral teacher. Nor do people mind Christians very much, provided that we mind our own business. No, what people dislike about Christianity is the exclusive claim of the crucified Christ. The only Christianity they will accept is based on a Christ without a cross.

LESSON 11

WALKING BY THE SPIRIT

Galatians 5:13–26

THE BIG PICTURE

Paul has been preaching the glorious gospel of grace to the Galatian believers and warning them against any teaching that would add works of the law to the finished work of Jesus Christ on the cross. He has been calling the Galatian Christians to embrace their freedom in Christ, rather than returning to the slavery of life under the law (Gal. 5:1). But Paul knows one objection that his opponents will raise in response to his emphasis on freedom: this kind of preaching is dangerous, they will say, because it can easily lead to licentious and sinful living. So, in Galatians 5:13–26, Paul explains more fully the kind of freedom in which true Christians walk. It is not a freedom that provides opportunities for sinful living and the pursuit of evil pleasure! It is a freedom that is linked to the very Spirit of God; believers in Jesus "walk by the Spirit" (v. 16) and are led by him, rather than by their own flesh. In fact, true freedom in Christ comes as believers in him begin to display "the fruit of the Spirit" (v. 22)—the natural outgrowth of the indwelling Spirit of God within followers of Christ. True gospel freedom is neither legalistic nor licentious; it is the freedom of being led by the Holy Spirit.

Read Galatians 5:13–26.

GETTING STARTED

1. Think about a time when you were given new freedom or a big responsibility. Perhaps it was the first time you were given a job, the first time you traveled to another state or country by yourself, or when you became a parent. What temptations accompanied that freedom and responsibility? What motivated you to steward the freedom or responsibility faithfully?

2. How is the Holy Spirit usually talked about in your church tradition? Do you think that the role of the Spirit in the Christian life is overemphasized? Underemphasized? Explain your answer.

OBSERVING THE TEXT

3. What repeated words or phrases does Paul use in this passage? What is new? What ideas has he already mentioned earlier in the letter?

Freedom of the Spirit, pg. 219

The only way to be free from fleshly desire is to be sanctified by God's Spirit. His influence alone can prevent liberty from degenerating into license, for "where the Spirit of the Lord is, there is freedom" (2 Cor. 3:17). The third member of the Trinity, one might say, is a "free" Spirit. He helps us hold on to our liberty without becoming either legalistic or licentious.

4. What is the significance of Paul's focus on the Spirit in this passage? Why is the Spirit so important in the life of the believer, and what do you sometimes forget about the role of the Holy Spirit in your life?

5. How does Paul describe the impact of the Spirit on the life of a true Christian? As you look over Galatians 5:13–26, note the ways that Christian lives are meant to be marked by walking by the Spirit.

UNDERSTANDING THE TEXT

6. Look at Galatians 5:13. How might Paul, in this verse, be anticipating an objection from his Jewish opponents to his gospel of grace? How does this verse, as well as the following one, help us to understand the true meaning of Christian freedom? What do verses 13–15 teach us about how faith in Christ impacts our relationships with one another?

7. In Galatians 5:16–18, what two ways of "walking" does Paul contrast? Why does he say that these two ways of living are opposed to each other? How does this teaching connect to what he has already taught the Galatian believers about the Old Testament law?

8. What observations can you make about what Paul chooses to include in his list of "the works of the flesh" (5:19–21)? What observations can you make about what he chooses to include in his list of "the fruit of the Spirit" (5:22–23)? What is the significance of his choice of words— "works" of the flesh and "fruit" of the Spirit? What is implied by the metaphor of "fruit"?

9. Why does Paul include the language of crucifixion with regard to the "flesh" of the Christian and its desires (5:24)? What does the picture of crucifixion imply about our desires, as well as our connection to Jesus Christ our Savior?

10. Note Paul's final instruction in this section: "Keep in step with the Spirit" (5:25). What is striking about the phrase "keep in step"? How might this metaphor guide us in the positive work of sanctification, as well as the negative work (putting off and fighting sin)? Why might Paul return to a horizontal application (how the Galatian believers treat one another) in verse 26, as the chapter ends?

The Spirit's Fruit, pg. 234

All the graces of the Spirit belong together, which perhaps explains why the word "fruit" occurs in the singular. The fruit of the Spirit is one whole spiritual life that is rooted in the one Spirit of God. To change the image for a moment, these virtues are not nine different gems, but nine different facets of the same dazzling jewel.

BIBLE CONNECTIONS

11. Read Romans 6:1–4. How does Paul's teaching in these verses parallel Galatians 5:13–18? What hints do you get that Paul might be anticipating similar pushback to his gospel preaching among the Jewish believers in Rome? Why is his response to potential objections so important— and so vital to the way we understand the grace of God in Christ?

12. In John 14:15–17, Jesus promises that the Holy Spirit, the "Helper," will come to the disciples to dwell with them and be with them forever. Read through those verses from John now. How does Jesus' promise about the Holy Spirit further inform our understanding of Paul's teaching in Galatians 5 about life in the Spirit?

THEOLOGY CONNECTIONS

13. The Westminster Confession of Faith says this about sanctification: "In which war, although the remaining corruption, for a time, may much prevail; yet, through the continual supply of strength from the sanctifying Spirit of Christ, the regenerate part doth overcome; and so, the saints grow in grace, perfecting holiness in the fear of God" (13.3). Why is it helpful to see sanctification as a war? How does this doctrinal statement remind us of the ultimate hope we have as Spirit-led followers of Jesus?

14. The Heidelberg Catechism says that the Holy Spirit "is also given to me, to make me by true faith share in Christ and all his benefits, to comfort me, and to remain with me forever" (Q&A 53). What is encouraging to you as you consider the gift of the indwelling Holy Spirit in your heart and life? How does this catechism answer further explain Paul's teaching about the Spirit in Galatians 5?

APPLYING THE TEXT

15. Perhaps you have been taught about the grace of God—and forgiveness through Christ—for many years. What tendencies have you detected in your own heart toward licentiousness or presuming on the grace of God? How can you fight against the sinful temptation to see God's grace as a license to sin more?

16. How is the fruit of the Spirit within you meant to impact your relationships with other people in your family, church, and community, according to this passage? Where do you see the need for personal growth in these relationships? Which fruit do you think is the most lacking in your life currently?

17. What might it look like for you to more intentionally "keep in step" with the Spirit (Gal. 5:25)? What means has God given us to maintain the vitality of our relationship with him? Why do we so often neglect an intentional nurturing of our relationship with God, by his Spirit, and how can we overcome these hindrances?

PRAYER PROMPT

The apostle Paul would surely say that there is no greater gift to the Christian than the indwelling Holy Spirit. Pray today that you would grow daily in the way that you "keep in step" with the Spirit in your walk with God. Ask God to nurture and grow each aspect of the "fruit" of the Spirit in your life, that you would more and more experience the true freedom of Christ in obedience to him.

Walking Daily with the Spirit, pg. 240

Keeping in step takes discipline, and so does spiritual growth. The Holy Spirit rarely works in extraordinary ways. Instead, he uses the ordinary means of grace to bring spiritual growth: the reading and preaching of God's Word, the sacraments of baptism and communion, and the life of prayer. Contrary to what so many Christians seem to believe, true spiritual growth does not come from some special experience of the Holy Spirit. Instead, it comes from walking with the Spirit every day.

LESSON 12

LIFE IN YOUR SPIRITUAL FAMILY

Galatians 6:1–10

THE BIG PICTURE

Paul has been moving in more and more of a practical and ethical direction as his letter to the Galatians progresses. Now, in chapter 6, he becomes even more detailed as he explains the implications of the gospel of Jesus Christ for life with one another in the body of Christ, the church. Those who have come to salvation in Jesus Christ by grace through faith alone are called to show grace to one another and bear each other's burdens, even as they call each other away from failure and sin. The church is meant to be a gracious and restorative community, shaped by the gospel and not by harshness and cruelty. Even so, Paul continues to warn the Galatian believers against having hearts that mock God by abandoning his gospel in any way. All people will reap what they sow! True, faith-filled followers of Jesus Christ are those who "sow" according to the Spirit of God, and this sowing bears fruit (among other things) in doing good to those in the spiritual family of God.

Read Galatians 6:1–10.

GETTING STARTED

1. "I'm spiritual, but I'm not religious." Have you ever heard someone say something like that? If so, what was the context? Often, an interest in spirituality apart from religion can mask a resistance to actually joining and being part of a community of faith, with all of the implications that come with that commitment. Why do you think pursuing spirituality on one's own might be more appealing to some people than joining with, and committing to, a community of faith?

2. In what ways have you observed people speaking or living in open mockery of God? Why ought this to break our hearts as followers of Jesus? How can hypocrisy within the church be just as much a mockery of God as blatant and overt disrespect for him and his Word? Where have you seen hypocrisy in, for example, the way in which those who identify as Christians treat each other?

The Community of Faith, pg. 244

The Holy Spirit does not produce this fruit for our private enjoyment. True spirituality is not an individualistic quest for self-fulfillment—the kind of thing one has to climb to the top of a pillar to discover. The life of the Spirit flourishes for the sake of others. It is not experienced in private, primarily, but exercised in public. Therefore, it does not grow in isolation, but within the community of faith.

OBSERVING THE TEXT

3. What seems to be the dominant theme, or big idea, in Galatians 6:1–6? Explain your answer. What is countercultural and even somewhat unnatural about the instructions in these verses?

4. How do verses 1–6 of Galatians 6 compare and contrast with verses 7–10? In what ways does Paul change his tone throughout the passage? Are there parts of this passage that seem confusing or even contradictory to you? Which ones?

5. What word pictures, illustrations, or metaphors does Paul use in Galatians 6:1–10? Why might he have chosen some of these particular images?

UNDERSTANDING THE TEXT

6. What important reminders about the body of Christ are present in Galatians 6:1? How does Paul speak about other members of the church? In what manner should we engage with another believer who has fallen

into sin? How can we guard ourselves, even as we seek to restore a fallen believer?

7. In what sense does bearing "one another's burdens" fulfill "the law of Christ" (Gal. 6:2)? What does Paul mean by that? How is Christ our ultimate example of bearing the burdens of others, and what are some ways in which our lives could demonstrate that we have truly understood and believed his burden-bearing work on our behalf?

8. In verses 3–5, what kind of attitude does Paul warn against? What does he mean by thinking we are "something," and why is such presumption so dangerous (v. 3)? How do these verses demonstrate the importance of humility, meekness, and personal devotion to Christ, even in the midst of life in community with others?

Keeping Christ's Law, pg. 249
One way to fulfill the law of love is to bear one another's burdens. By caring for one another, we become law-abiding Christians. Of course, we are not saved by keeping the law. However, God's will for our lives, as expressed in his moral law, has not changed. Now that we have been saved, we must keep the law of Christ . . . [by] bearing one another's burdens, just as Christ showed his love for us when he bore the burden of our sin on the cross.

9. What metaphor or word picture does Paul utilize in Galatians 6:7–9? Why do you think he chooses this illustration? How does it relate to what he wrote earlier in this letter? What kind of thinking and/or behavior is he warning the Galatian believers against?

10. What does sowing "to the Spirit" look like, in contrast to sowing to the flesh (6:8)? How does one know if he or she is sowing to the Spirit, or sowing to his or her own flesh? How might verses 9–10 of this passage help us, at least initially, to answer that question?

BIBLE CONNECTIONS

11. Read James 5:20. How do James and Paul agree on the right treatment of a sinner in the community of faith? Why is a gentle rebuke, with restoration, so glorious and beautiful in the church?

12. In 1 Corinthians 5:9–13, Paul speaks of sin in the church at Corinth. Based on your reading of that passage, as well as your study of Galatians 6:1–10, what instances of sin in the church does Paul seem to be

addressing in each place? What calls for restoration, and what calls for separation? How do these passages help us recognize the difference?

THEOLOGY CONNECTIONS

13. While the Presbyterian Church in America's *Book of Church Order* (*BCO*) does not hold the same weight as the Westminster Confession of Faith, it is founded on biblical principles, which its authors sought to apply to every area of church life. The *BCO* defines the goals of church discipline as seeking to bring about (1) the glory of God, (2) the purity of the church, and (3) the reclamation of the sinner. How might Galatians 6:1–10 guide church leaders during the process of rebuke or even the formal discipline of a church member? How might this passage have influenced the way that the three goals of church discipline were phrased in the *BCO*?

14. John Calvin wrote: "To *sow to the flesh*, is to look forward to the wants of the present life, without any regard to a future life" (*Commentary on Galatians*, on 6:8). How were the Judaizers guilty of sowing to the flesh with regard to their hope for salvation? What are some ways that people sow to the flesh in our culture today, according to Calvin's explanation?

APPLYING THE TEXT

15. What are some ways that you are tempted to respond to sin wrongly in the context of the church? How have you observed the painful results of people in the community of faith responding to sin in sinful ways? How can you prepare to be a person who graciously restores brothers or sisters who have fallen into sin?

16. Paul warns against many dangerous ways of thinking and acting in this passage: thinking too highly of ourselves, being harsh with others, comparing ourselves to others, deceiving ourselves as we mock God, and so on. Which of Paul's warnings was most convicting to you as you follow Jesus and engage with the church? Why? What attitudes and actions need to change for you to grow in this area?

Sowing to the Spirit, pg. 261
Whoever sows to the Spirit reaps the richest harvest of all: eternal life. This does not mean, of course, that salvation comes by works. Eternal life is a gift that is based on believing, not on doing. However, believers are doers, and although no one is ever saved by works, no one is ever saved without them either. Therefore, having been saved by grace, the believer goes out and sows to please the Spirit.

17. How might you be able to begin to self-diagnose the tendency you have to "sow to the flesh" rather than to "sow to the Spirit"? In what ways does your treatment of others in the community of faith serve as a reflection and indication of the health of your relationship with God? Where do you need to grow most, right now, in your loving goodness to those in "the household of faith" (6:10)?

PRAYER PROMPT

There are many implications for life as believers in the context of the church that emerge from this passage. As you close your time of study, consider just one or two of these implications, and commit them to prayer. You could pray for a spirit of gentleness as you seek to restore fallen brothers or sisters. Or you could ask God for strength to bear the burdens of others with more joy and humility. Take time, now, and pray.

LESSON 13

GLORY IN THE CROSS

Galatians 6:11–18

THE BIG PICTURE

Paul concludes his letter to the Galatians by calling their attention to the fact that he writes these final verses with his own hand—that is, without the help of his scribe (6:11). He wants these Christians to know that he is thoughtfully, carefully, and personally concluding his letter to them. In these final verses are familiar themes: Paul warns against the Judaizers who would seek to add circumcision as a requirement for all believers, notes the hypocrisy and ironic lawlessness of his opponents, and calls attention to his focus on the cross of Christ alone, which has brought him great suffering and persecution. The Galatian believers are left with a clear and powerful concluding call: boast in the gospel of Jesus Christ—and nothing else! The true apostle who writes to them bears the marks of suffering for the gospel in his own body, and he is intent on protecting their gospel faith and guarding it against any other supposed gospel.

Read Galatians 6:11–18.

GETTING STARTED

1. What are some memorable examples that you have witnessed of people bragging about their accomplishments or capabilities? How do some

111

people boast overtly? How do other people find more subtle ways to draw attention to themselves?

2. Consider some leaders or activists in history who have been doggedly and stubbornly focused on one narrow goal. Who comes to mind? What was their overriding objective? How would you characterize the specific focus of the life and ministry of the apostle Paul?

OBSERVING THE TEXT

3. As you read through Galatians 6:11–18, what struck you about the way in which Paul concludes this letter? What does he emphasize the most? What points and lessons from earlier in his letter does he repeat in these final verses?

More Than a Postscript, pg. 270

The last section of Galatians, therefore, is more than a hastily written postscript, the afterthought of an apostle. Instead, these verses constitute a summary of the entire letter. They place circumcision over against the cross, showing that justification by grace alone, through faith alone, in Christ alone means boasting in the cross alone.

4. You may have noticed the theme of circumcision again in this passage. How and why does Paul mention this religious ritual again, and why might he find it necessary to do so?

5. How do Paul's tone and language in writing to the Galatians in the final verses of the letter compare to his tone and language in the opening verses of it? Why do you think this is the case?

UNDERSTANDING THE TEXT

6. Look again at Galatians 6:12–13. Why might those pushing for circumcision be motivated by the avoidance of persecution? On what basis does Paul say that they might be persecuted? What do these verses tell us about the motivation of the Judaizers?

7. What does Paul imply in verse 13 about the Judaizers' overall commitment to the Old Testament law? How does he point out their hypocrisy with regard to their obsession with circumcision?

8. How has Paul, in the letter to the Galatians, boasted only in the cross of Christ (6:14)? How is this contrasted with the boasting, misbehavior, and false gospel of his opponents? What does Paul mean by saying that "the world" has been crucified to him, and he to the world (v. 14)? Why is this such an important reality for Christians to understand as they follow Jesus Christ?

9. In verse 15, how does Paul move beyond debates about circumcision and uncircumcision to a higher and more important reality about Christians? What does he say is most important? What does he mean by "a new creation"? How did he explain this reality earlier in his letter? See Galatians 2:19-20

10. How does Paul again link himself to Jesus Christ and the true gospel in verse 17? In what way does this statement connect to what he has already argued in chapters 1–2? Why might he conclude this letter with another reminder of his apostleship and suffering for the gospel of Jesus Christ?

BIBLE CONNECTIONS

11. In Galatians 6:11–18, Paul ends his letter by again confronting the "gospel-plus" teaching that plagued the Galatian believers, as they dealt with Judaizers who insisted on circumcision as an essential rite of true faith. Take a moment to read Acts 15:1–11. How does Peter respond to the Jewish insistence on circumcision at the Jerusalem Council? What key points does he make about the salvation and inclusion of the Gentiles, and how do his words echo Paul's words in Galatians?

12. Take a moment to read Mark 10:17–22, the account of a rich young man who approaches Jesus to ask him a crucial question. In what does this man seem to boast? How does he seek to justify himself? What does Jesus identify as the main thing that is keeping him from true repentance and faith?

Boasting in the Cross, pg. 275
Paul was always boasting about the cross . . . and God forbid that he should ever boast about anything else. Christ crucified meant the world to him, as it should to us. The cross is not just *something* to boast about; it is the *only thing* to boast about. The cross is the only thing to boast about because it means that God loves us enough to die for us, that he saved us through the death of his own dear Son.

THEOLOGY CONNECTIONS

13. John Knox, who is sometimes known as "the Father of the Scottish Reformation," once reflected on his life and ministry with these words: "I sought neither preeminence, glory, nor riches; my honor was that Jesus Christ should reign." How do Knox's words echo those of Paul in Galatians 6:11–18? How can Knox's commitment become a model for our Christian lives?

14. Q&A 49 of the Westminster Larger Catechism speaks of Jesus Christ and his astounding humiliation on the cross for our sins. Here is how Jesus' work of humility is described: "Christ humbled himself in his death, in that having been betrayed by Judas, forsaken by his disciples, scorned and rejected by the world, condemned by Pilate, and tormented by his persecutors; having also conflicted with the terrors of death, and the powers of darkness, felt and borne the weight of God's wrath, he laid down his life an offering for sin, enduring the painful, shameful, and cursed death of the cross." What causes you to wonder when you consider the work of Jesus Christ on the cross? What truths articulated in this catechism question put to shame any human effort that would seek to merit salvation? How does this passage from the catechism help you to understand better the appropriate call to "boast" in the cross of Jesus Christ—and nothing else?

APPLYING THE TEXT

15. As you examine your actions and words as a follower of Jesus, do you find that you are at times tempted not to fully live out the gospel, in order to avoid forms of persecution, embarrassment, or hardship? In what life situations do you find these temptations to be especially strong?

16. In what are you tempted to "boast"—either overtly or privately—apart from the cross of Christ? How can you grow in your commitment to boast only in the cross of Christ, as Paul does?

17. How are you tempted to get bogged down in debates about trivial matters related to your faith, the church, and Christian controversies? In what ways can you remind yourself and others about the importance of life as "new creations," born of the Spirit, and walking by faith as followers of Jesus?

United with Christ, pg. 280
The marks of Jesus may seem disgraceful to the world, but they are precious in the sight of God. They are so precious, in fact, that on occasion Paul prayed for the privilege of becoming so united to Christ that he would come to share in his sufferings.

PRAYER PROMPT

As you close your time of studying this passage, and also the book of Galatians as a whole, take some time to pray about your own commitment to the gospel of Jesus Christ by faith alone. Ask God to protect you from the influence of "gospel-plus" teachings, which would seek to add your works to the finished work of Jesus. Pray that God would give you grace to boast in the cross of his Son alone, in whom you have full salvation and membership in the family of God.

Jon Nielson is senior pastor of Spring Valley Presbyterian Church in Roselle, Illinois, and the author of *Bible Study: A Student's Guide*, among other books. He has served in pastoral positions at Holy Trinity Church, Chicago, and College Church, Wheaton, Illinois, and as director of training for the Charles Simeon Trust.

Philip Graham Ryken (DPhil, University of Oxford) is president of Wheaton College. He teaches the Bible for the Alliance of Confessing Evangelicals, speaking nationally on the radio program *Every Last Word*, and is the author of a number of books and commentaries.

Did you enjoy this Bible study? Consider writing a review online.
The authors appreciate your feedback!

Or write to P&R at editorial@prpbooks.com with your comments.
We'd love to hear from you.